LEO
Thru the Numbers

Paul & Valeta Rice

SAMUEL WEISER, INC.
York Beach, Maine 03910

First published in 1983 by
Samuel Weiser, Inc.
P.O. Box 612
York Beach, Maine 03910

Copyright © 1983 by Paul and Valeta Rice

All rights reserved. No part of this book may be reproduced in any form or by any means, without permission in writing from the publisher.

ISBN 0-87728-569-1 (Leo)

Library of Congress Catalog Card Number: 82-63004

Typeset by Deerfield Printing Company
Printed by Mitchell-Shear, Inc.

People wishing to contact the authors may write them at the following address:

Paul and Valeta Rice
F.A.C.E. Association
177 Webster Street, Suite A-105
Monterey, Ca. 93940

Contents

Authors 4
When? 5
Leo 7
How to Compute Your Destiny 9
Destiny Number 1 11
Destiny Number 2 12
Destiny Number 3 13
Destiny Number 4 14
Destiny Number 5 15
Destiny Number 6 16
Destiny Number 7 17
Destiny Number 8 18
Destiny Number 9 19
Destiny Number 11 20
Destiny Number 22 21
Destiny Number 33 22
Destiny Number 44 23
Destiny Number 55 24
Destiny Number 66 25
Your Personal Chart 26
Personal Year 27
Personal Month 27
Table of Personal Months 28
Challenges of Life 33
Table of Challenges 34
Numbers 36
Bibliography 40

AUTHORS

If Valeta and Paul Rice sound familiar, it may be because of their extensive travel to many cities from Fairbanks, Alaska all the way down the coast to San Diego, California, and across the continental United States to Baltimore, Maryland. During their invitational stopovers they conduct workshops and seminars about Name Analysis and Birthdate Analysis, traveling together for over twenty years.

The Rices have been interested in occult studies for over forty years, starting with the receipt of the book on ESP from Duke University. Their search for esoteric knowledge carried them into Astrology, Reincarnation, Palmistry, Tarot, Color, Music, I Ching, ESP, Dream Analysis, the Qabala, Yoga, Structural Dynamics, meditation/visualization/healing and many more sciences. Their Socratic and regression techniques have been rewarding to clients.

While their professions are different (Valeta is a minister and psychic counselor, Paul is a professional engineer), they enjoy the cooperation that team teaching provides. Each summer they travel wherever they are invited to teach Name Analysis and Birthdate Analysis as well as conducting private sessions by appointment.

Their major work, now in its second printing, is concerned with name analysis and is a book called *POTENTIAL!*, which is available at many book stores or can be ordered directly from the authors.

A second work, called *TIMING*, is a book dealing with birthdate analysis for all the birth signs.

WHEN?

When shall I start my next project?
When should I ask for a raise?
When should I sign that contract?
When should I get married?
How will I feel when I retire?

How many times has a person looked for an answer to these questions? During this modern age the veil has been lifted on the ancient science of the vibration of the NUMBERS. This ancient science, known as the *metaphysical science of numerology*, was developed by Pythagoras, who lived in the sixth century B.C.

The simplicity of NUMEROLOGY is astounding. If you can count on your fingers you can use Numerology. It requires only a few hours study before you can begin to put to use the basic facts that you have acquired. This knowledge will give one the opportunity to see himself and other acquaintances in a better light. Apparently its simplicity is the reason Numerology was used less than other occult sciences in the past, and our society today seems to prefer complexity also.

Surprisingly, the knowledge of the numbers which govern your life will reveal many things you already know, that you had suspected or you had hoped were true.

The Numerologist takes his place alongside the Astrologer, Graphologist, Palmist and the Tarot reader, who all believe that we came into this life, not by chance, but by choice, and from these arts or sciences much can be revealed about a person's life.

Numerology reveals the vibrations in many categories including the number connected to the Birth Date, the Personal Year, the Personal Month and how the planet vibrations correlate to these numbers.

The awareness of the numbers connected to these categories helps us with a yearly and monthly course to follow.

Everyone wants to be happy and prosperous. Many unfortunate people have not learned to harmonize their birthdate vibrations with the timing of their decisions.

We are constantly called upon to make decisions which may make significant changes in our lives. Often we make the wrong decisions over family, friends, or in business because our "TIMING" is off.

The simple system of the vibration of the numbers and how they pertain to your life and the timing of your decisions will help you to come to logically deduced insights and, if carefully followed, will make you increasingly happy and prosperous throughout your lifetime.

Pythagoras, who lived twenty-five centuries ago, is considered the Father of Numbers. It is believed that he received his knowledge of the occult value of the numbers while in Egypt and Babylon. He taught these concepts and many more in his School of Occult Philosophy where the few who were allowed to attend learned how "everything can be related to numbers."

The Science of Numerology is not a quick way to happiness and achievement; it is only by becoming aware of your favorable number vibrations and then changing the unfavorable vibrations that you can smooth your pathway.

Numbers live and numbers tell and everyone can become aware of their vibrations and their relationship to themselves through the numbers.

We have explored the mundane and esoteric values of the numbers and their relationship to astrology with a lot of help from our guides.

This knowledge we wish to share with you.

MAHALO!
(Thank you!)

LEO

July 21st to August 21st FIXED/FIRE

The LION Ruler: SUN

The LION symbolizes the King, the ruler by divine right (he thinks). The Lion, who belongs to the cat family, can be soft and cuddly, purring away on your lap as he gently digs his claws into your thighs (ouch!), then tires of the game and jumps down to pursue game he can stalk.

Leo is like the cat, independent, full of pride, roaring when he doesn't get his own way, then purring and smiling and petting you until he wins his objective.

Leo has a commanding air, carries himself with pride, is not easy to ignore in a crowd—and maybe better you should not ignore him for you will be detracting from his outgoing radiance. This regal manner of the Leo brings up the tone of a crowd. We all stand straighter when faced with a Leo, for we instinctively recognize authority in him. We are using the masculine pronoun for Leo is a male sign.

The WILL, individualized by Leo, is the spirit of power and vitality directed toward bringing light and energy to others. He is faithful to those he loves and does not change his affections easily.

He is loyal to his associates. Don't betray a Leo or he will roar, destroying your ego. He can't understand why you should not follow his direction when he is so good to you, supplying you with money (that you earn), food, superb wines, excellent entertainment, and encompassing love to shelter you from all ill-will.

Here is the organizer of splendid projects, the fun loving, generous and courageous person whom most people love to follow, for he is the king of beasts, unafraid to charge ahead into the unknown, bringing success to his followers as well.

PARTNERS: There is no particular birth sign that can easily be ruled by Leo. One would think that the feminine sign, Taurus, Cancer, Virgo, Scorpio, Capricorn or Pisces would be compatible with this male energy but each of these has its own peculiarity by which it rules its own nature. Cancer and Pisces being sensitive, compassionate signs, would understand a Leo better if they were not totally inundated by Leo's powerful influence. They COULD tame him (her) with soft love and flattery. Leos love to have people appreciate their reliability and deep love.

SUN: Rules the self-consciousness, the self-respect that is inherent in Leo. He has the courage and integrity to move into areas where angels fear to tread. In doing so he breaks established barriers so that others can follow and reap the benefits. He is honest and direct as the Sun is direct, shining on everyone who comes within range. His space includes as far as he can see, hear or imagine!

FIXED: This is Leo's aspect of force manifesting in matter. This is active power, visible and unswervingly stubborn when he decides on the path he wants to take to achieve his goals.

FIRE: These are the virtues you brought with you from former lifetimes. This fire of the inner heart surges forth to bring success and love to everyone, if the Leo is on his way to being evolved. The Leo destiny is a high one, reaching to the Sun, leading and becoming the servant at the same time. Vital and warm.

NEGATIVE VIBRATIONS: Brusque; dominion over others; powerful enemy; arrogance; vain; ego; careless; sloppy.

NUMBERS: The NUMBER that is connected to Leo's BIRTH SIGN increases or decreases Leo's energy. Wherever you find Leo in your chart look at the influence your DESTINY NUMBER has on this house in your horoscope.

HOW TO COMPUTE YOUR DESTINY

Your DESTINY, sometimes called the LIFE PATH, is the road that you as an individual travel. This is why you are here, what you should be doing in this lifetime in order to fulfill your soul. The NUMBER combined with your LEO BIRTH SIGN reveals your soul urge, your reason for incarnating this lifetime. If you do not follow your DESTINY, you can become frustrated with unresolved goals.

Each month is represented by a number:

JANUARY	1	APRIL	4	JULY	7	OCTOBER	1
FEBRUARY	2	MAY	5	AUGUST	8	NOVEMBER	2
MARCH	3	JUNE	6	SEPTEMBER	9	DECEMBER	3

Write your BIRTHDATE on your PERSONAL CHART, page 26, using the NAME of your month—July or August—not the number of the month. Be sure to use the full year, *i.e.*, 1935, NOT '35; or 1940, NOT '40, or whatever is the year of your birth. We use the "1" in the year, i.e., 1935, 1966, 1940, as well as the rest of the numbers.

On scratch paper add the number of the month, the day of the month and the year of your birth together, then reduce this number by constantly adding the numbers together until you come to a single digit or a MASTER NUMBER.

The MASTER NUMBERS are **11, 22, 33, 44, 55** and **66**.

EXAMPLE: July 30, 1960 (1+9+6+0 = 16; 1+6 = 7)
7   3   7   = 17; 1+7 = **8**

EXAMPLE: Aug. 8, 1957
8   8   22/4   = 38; 3+8 = **11**; 1+1 = **2**

EXAMPLE: Aug. 12, 1957
8   3   22/4   = **33** or **33/6**

Experiment with your birthdate and see if you can come up with a "hidden" MASTER NUMBER.

We call the second and third examples *Research and Discovery* since we have found a *hidden* Master Number. When the Master Numbers are hidden an unexpected talent lies in the direction of the vibration of that particular number.

So, Leo, every time you find a **1, 4, 6** or **8** in your birth sign or someone else's birth sign try all these methods. Then you find out if you or another person is vibrating on the Master Number or the single digit. There are persons who are content to vibrate and work on the single digit pulsation and put their talents to excellent use in that position rather than try for the esoteric vibration of the Master Numbers. This depends a lot on other numbers which concern several other categories in numerology.

The main purpose of finding your DESTINY NUMBER is to realize where you are in life's stream and learn to flow with it.

The DESTINY NUMBER and your BIRTH SIGN are two things that you cannot change. You were born on a certain day, month, and year, for you chose to be here at that time to experience what you have come to this lifetime to learn.

Another way to research and discover if you have a hidden Master Number is to add this way:

July 28, 1919 = 7 + 28 + 1919 (1 + 9 + 1 + 9 = 20) = **55/1**
August 1, 1938 = 8 + 1 + 19 + 38   = **66** or **3**
August 31, 1940 = 8 + 31 + 5 (1 + 9 + 4 + 0 = 14; 1 + 4 = 5)
    8   31   5   = **44** or **8**

We always show the single digit that the Master Number reduces to in order to see which level a person vibrates on.

The following pages will interpret the number that you have chosen to go with your birth sign for this lifetime.

DESTINY NUMBER 1

This **1** Destiny Number gives you even more impetus to create your own world or kingdom, Leo. This creative force helps you to charge ahead with innovative projects and original ideas.

The fire of ambition erupts into a moving force that assists others to inaugurate ideas beyond their original concept. You are helping others to turn on creative ability they may not be aware of. This is why Leos make good teachers for they inspire students to better performances.

You would do well in the entertainment world as a director of plays and movies and TV documentaries. Once an idea has taken hold for expression on film or in live performances it will be hard to dislodge you from your viewpoint. "Live performances" could mean action in your own family, also. You want to go to the theatre and your family wants to go to the beach; you KNOW that the theatre will give your family more ideas than playing in the sand. Take a good look at what you are insisting on; is the play at the theatre instructive or would playing in the sand give your family time for restful reflection?

1 brings success because of your optimistic outlook. Yves Saint Laurent, the designer, knew that given an opportunity, he could become a world-famous designer—and he did. Confidence in your own creative ideas will bring the same or similar success.

NEGATIVE: You could be forcing your will onto others without their permission. Also, it is not easy for a **1** Leo to accept ideas from others. Could this be a lack of courage? The quavering inside, the arrogance showing outside?

Number 1

Color: Red—for energy. Project this to others.
Element: Fire—more energy. Take your vitamins.
Musical Note: C—the self-starter.

DESTINY NUMBER 2

This is not the easiest Destiny Number for you, Leo, as it requires all of your patience to pursue your goals. It means using diplomacy to get your desires, listening and not reacting immediately when presented with ideas contrary to your own. Though you chose to come into this lifetime to be the ruler, you cannot rule by force under this vibration. Get the cooperation of your associates by using your leonine charm and wit. Your sex appeal (whether male or female) will garner your wishes faster than pounding your shoe on the table.

The intuitive aspect of this number can be used to counsel others by sending your intense vibrations (positive, we hope) across whatever distance to another person or group. Others will feel your energy although it is unspoken, and will react in like manner. This means if you send positive creative ideas across, they will react with positive ideas—unless the person receiving the energy is wallowing in his own "poor me" stew so much it would take several gradient sessions to raise him to the level of listening to what is being sent or said.

When speaking to groups or your family, smile a lot. Give to your friends and associates as you like to be given and complimented. There lies your secret of success in this number.

NEGATIVE: Your impatience does get the better of you. Scream and rant by yourself, throw rocks, run or swim or do some exercise that will extinguish these negative vibrations. You do have the power to get what and where you want if you exercise a little caution in this diplomatic vibration. Jacqueline Onassis hasn't done so badly for herself, has she?

Number 2

Color: Orange—for balance and harmony.
Element: Water—dealing with emotions.
Musical Note: *D*—for harmony and tranquility.

DESTINY NUMBER 3

Leos love to have center stage, and be the object of everyone's attention. This is the lifetime when you can exercise this feeling of being the entertainer, the one who provides laughs and good humor in any gathering. Let yourself go! Relax! as the song goes. **3** is the joy of living; perhaps you are here on earth this lifetime for a vacation!

If you are working harder than you think necessary, perhaps you are vibrating on the "strength" of the **3**. **3** contains the creativity (**1**) and the diplomacy (**2**) which leads to the outpouring activity of **3**. The creating you are doing, whether it is on the positive or negative side takes energy (**3**). Energy is also involved in playing the diplomatic role.

You can take the ideas suggested to you, Leo (if you are in a listening mood) and carry them to fruition with your usual action-oriented energy.

Communication is the keyword for this Destiny Number. Talking, listening, exchanging ideas, entertaining your clients, your boss and any other road or avenue you can think of will bring results in the near future. Advertise your talents, your business, your worth to your family. Use your talent for words, learn another language. Pursue knowledge as a lion pursues his game.

Esoterically you can remember your dreams and establish contact with higher beings, if you desire.

NEGATIVE: Since you love to be the center of attention it is hard to guard against overacting. Your excessive energy can wear people down. The opposite of this would be a lack of energy to carry through your purposes. If this is true, check carefully and see what is causing this, for a "not caring" attitude is not natural for you as a **3**. Even problems shouldn't affect you for long. If you find yourself just dabbling in life, are you playing the cowardly lion???

Number **3**

Color: Yellow—for expression.
Element: Fire—for energy.
Musical Note: E—for feeling.

DESTINY NUMBER 4

There must be a product, something you can touch, see, feel or handle to make the best use of this **4** Destiny Number, Leo. There is an esoteric side for manifesting what you want, yet these manifestations are usually on the practical side. You are already one whom people look to for guidance, for your clear thinking mind sees solutions (on the practical side again) and remedies for many problems and challenges.

Since you are orderly and devoted to duty, your patience may be a little short with those who are careless and inconsistent in their work. You won't waste time with these types of people for you value your time and your talents to such a degree that using your energy to straighten out the problems of careless people is a waste of your valuable time and space.

You will endure hardships because you can see the rewards when the task is complete. Then you can bask in the sunshine of adulation for a job well done.

Though you have a good sense of timing and humor, you are not amenable to practical jokes, especially about yourself. The lion roars when upset but purrs when stroked.

Your love interests are clearly defined in this number. You always enjoy ruling and in a **4** you are not interested in being ruled. Your mate or lover can enjoy the adoration you give him/her as long as you come first.

NEGATIVE: Your thoroughness, exactness and self-discipline can become directed toward others to your detriment, as they will see only rigidity to your purposes and goals. Too much rigidity makes you stiff and clumsy in your approach to others.

Number **4**

Color: A beautiful, healing green—project this color to people from your heart.
Element: Earth—the stable person.
Musical Note: *F*—for construction, building, and making things strong and lasting.

DESTINY NUMBER 5

5 Destiny Number is a type of freedom, Leo. You are unstuck from the average humdrum life and can move freely in many directions if you take advantage of the adventurous vibrations that **5** has. This number means travel, either actually by boat, train or plane or travel in your mind or spirit. There are opportunities for you in many strange places. You do not have to seek adventure—it will come to you, changing your stated plans, bringing excitement into your life that was totally unexpected.

Many of the changes in your life may seem difficult since they involve friends and family. You will be seeing people differently as you absorb new ideas through studies in which you become involved.

You can be the world's best salesperson, Leo, with the ability to sell the beautiful, the quality items. Use the sensual approach in promoting your products.

Although inherently you are a faithful mate and lover, you have a roving eye with this Destiny Number. Since variety is the spice of life you may find yourself delving into the mysteries of several intriguing affairs with the opposite sex before you "settle down" and become devoted to one person.

NEGATIVE: Selfishness rears its ugly head when the negative vibrations take action. Since you want so much diversification you might indulge in drink, overeating, dope or some such stimulant. This will only bring in false pictures and thought forms which will lead you away from your goals.

Number **5**

Color: Turquoise—like a refreshing breeze.
Element: Air—the breath of life.
Musical Note: *G*—denoting change.

DESTINY NUMBER 6

As a **6** you make a wonderful loving parent, Leo. Your children may come under a strict disciplinary regime with you, which is no deterent to love. We all need a modicum of discipline to learn and understand where our parameters are, how far we can go in a certain circumstance without incurring the wrath of the gods. If children do not know the rules of kindness, courtesy and love, how can they grow up to be loving and kind adults?

This love moves on to include your mate, your friends, your associates, and the world. This is the number of the cosmic mother, who embraces all levels of consciousness and nurtures those on all levels. If you go into socially conscious professions you will be the one to carry the flag, lead strikes for better working conditions, and be in the front in the demonstrations for equality.

As a Leo you have the strength of the lion to help you stride ahead in your chosen profession. You have the will to succeed in creating harmony in this **6**. Sometimes justice or judgement does not seem in harmony, yet true justice means being fair and judging by using well-founded reason.

NEGATIVE: The mental approach to reaching a fair decision when faced with disciplinary action is better than letting your feeling of superiority goad you into making a rash judgement. Think it through before acting. You could be interfering in others' lives. The anxiety you feel about your family could make you bossy and nosy and, in general, a nuisance.

Number **6**

Color: Royal blue—for stability. Meditate on this color.
Element: Earth—responsibility to self and others.
Musical Note: A—for receptivity, harmony.

DESTINY NUMBER 7

Your ruler, the Sun—or radiance as we prefer to call it—is the fire of wisdom that you use from past experience to project into the future, Leo. This analytical number gives you the opportunity to search for your successes and mistakes in the past. As you search for past successes to build on to secure a better future, you also encounter the mistakes. You can reverse these mistakes and make them solid building blocks for a secure future. What was done was done, now how can you analyze that situation to make it profitable—or not let it happen again?

On the esoteric level 7s are the mystics who can heal spiritual gaps in a person's aura. Remember that permission must be asked of the person YOU feel needs healing, Leo. You are apt to go around TELLING others of your power which, of course, reduces the energy. Let this healing power come through you as you project this beautiful violet color to those who ask.

This perfect occult number is the bridge from the mundane to the esoteric, from the known to the unknown; from knowledge to performance.

Your mate or lover needs patience to understand your "in-depth" contemplation. This need to be quiet and contemplative is not compatible with responsibility to family. As a Leo you have enough stability of character to overcome this "priestly attitude" than some of the other signs, and can better adjust to functioning on this 7 level of consciousness (3rd dimensional) as well as furthering your studies in the metaphysical world.

NEGATIVE: You could become skeptical about the information you receive from higher dimensions and try to ignore this knowledge. Or you could remain aloof and uncaring and be difficult to communicate with.

Number 7

Color: Violet—which stands for reverence.
Element: Water—flowing with your knowledge.
Musical Note: B—for reflection on the past.

DESTINY NUMBER 8

8 symbolizes money, power and glory, and all this can be yours, Leo, if your foundation has been laid with care, study and honesty. If you climb over or step on the "little people" to get to the top, your underpinnings will become very shaky. We all get what we deserve.

Handling this power, this primal energy, becomes a study in the correct posture to hold the reins of those wild horses of success. The fire of your ambition and the courage of the lion will carry you far in your endeavors.

You operate in present time in this number, taking care of your daily decisions with full attention centered on the immediate project. You live in the NOW with **8**, planning for the future, of course, but using most of your energy to make your plans work in the present.

On the esoteric level you have the opportunity to open or reopen your third eye during this lifetime if you wish to follow the metaphysical teachings.

In this world, finance, government and industry are the best outlets for your energy. Large corporations need Leos who are willing to charge ahead with confidence to organize and use the potential of those employed by the company. If you choose the arts you can become famous as a dancer, painter, or sculptor, or in any field you choose. Lucille Ball became famous by using this **8** Leo energy, this urge to get ahead, to succeed.

You will attract many of the opposite sex to you, Leo, for your shining success is a beacon of light and energy for others.

NEGATIVE: If you scheme to get ahead with negative thoughts you will attract vibrations that will come and sit on your doorstep later to haunt you. Be careful in your selection of employees and those who have influence to further your career. Your ego could get away from you if you become greedy and abuse those "beneath" you.

NUMBER 8

Color: Rose—for love.
Element: Earth—for achievement, material gain.
Musical Note: High C—for striving.

DESTINY NUMBER 9

This is an achievement and success number for you, Leo. **9** means completion, finishing your job, your cycle of work, your cycles of thinking and planning. Those projects started some time ago are awaiting your attention, and when they are finished you will feel a surge of energy. This energy can be used on many projects. When things are unfinished the energy they contain hangs over us like a heavy cloud.

9 also means brotherly love, the concern for mankind in general. **9**s go beyond self to expand horizons, able in time to transcend bias or prejudice against other races or belief systems. When you reach the positive side of this number it will touch a responsive chord of recognition in vast numbers of people.

The destiny of the **9** is working in the mainstream of life where you can be an instrument for good. You would do well, Leo, as a civic worker, a reformer, composer of uplifting music or writer of philosophical treatises. You would also make a wonderful teacher.

Align yourself with a mate or lover who understands that you are on call to help your friends in need, no matter what the hour.

NEGATIVE: Since many people will come to you for advice and counselling, keep your vitamin pills handy so your energy is not depleted. The opposite of charitable attention is being unforgiving and the opposite of trust is being indiscreet. Think on these negative vibrations.

Number 9

Color: Yellow-gold—for perfection, the desire to make everything perfect, even people.
Element: Fire—for warmth, cuddling up to. People gravitate to where you are as they feel the warmth and the caring that you have.
Musical Note: High *D*—for accomplishment.

DESTINY NUMBER 11

You are the intelligent idealist who governs yourself so well that you are seldom cornered into action against your principles, Leo.

Your sign (Leo) is the one that can assist you to put your dreams into action. Your inner self is constantly urging you to create a better world, better inventions and better understanding between nations. The understanding between nations starts with understanding between me and thee, spreading to groups and thence to mankind.

This striving for perfection in yourself and your ideals assists you to project your radiance to others. They can see the wisdom in the goals that you propose and though they may fight against this idealistic aim they are only doing so because of the seeming threat to their survival.

In our industrial society, workers were able to have more goods and higher wages until the whole system became greedy. With greediness comes collapse of the system. You can bring back quality to industry by leading the people back to sanity of purpose.

Your magnetic personality draws people to you, including the opposite sex. A **1**, **3**, or a **5** Destiny Number would provide impetus and expansion to your doubly creative essence.

NEGATIVE: Leo, the Lion, with fixed ideas on how to change the world, charging ahead with banners flying, could turn into the fanatic, the one who MAKES people do what he/she wants them to do. The other negative vibration is holding onto all these ideals and refusing to share knowledge. This demand for perfection could make a Leo feel superior to the little people and turn Leo into a cynic.

Number **11**

Color: Silver—for attraction.
Element: Air—for the idealist.
Musical Note: High *E*—for magnetism.

DESTINY NUMBER 22

This is another good number for you, Leo, as it expresses your practicality, your mastery of the physical in yourself and in your surroundings.

You can put into practice the idealism of the **11** as it is contained in the **22** (**11** + **11** = **22**). This need for perfection is carried into action on your projects, whether they be ideas or concrete buildings. You want it done right! There is no carelessness or sloppiness allowed if you are in charge of the job. You have already learned that it is easier to do it right the first time, rather than go back and do it over.

There is diplomacy built into this number also, Leo. The double 2 gives you added strength to put your ideas across with proper words and gestures. You are dramatic!

You could head toward an international direction in government or politcs, direct large corporations or succeed in some form of communications work.

As a lover or mate you would be dynamic, as you have control of your physical self. Team up with an **11** Capricorn, Leo, and see sparks fly!

Spiritually you can be a strong force to build and support a belief system that is based on logic. Your magnificent dream of peace and prosperity for everyone is inherent in this belief.

NEGATIVE: Your base of operations may be limited if you are working on the negative side of this number with fixed ideas of how things should be done. Sometimes we need to compromise a little. If you do not follow through with your grandiose plans you become the big talker, not doer.

Number **22**

Color: Red-gold—for practical wisdom, using the things you have learned for practical application.
Element: Water—for cleansing. Clean out the fantasies from your life, see reality.
Musical Note: High *F*—for physical mastery.

DESTINY NUMBER 33

People are swayed by a good orator like you, Leo. You love to be in front, guiding others, being dramatic and holding your audience in the palm of your hand, which is tightly closed around your ideas. This flair for drama can sway many people, so watch your emotional control over them. You don't want more karma.

You can learn to experience many emotions and then share the knowledge of how to move vertically up the emotional ladder through hate, anxiety and anger, the minus factors, to the plus emotions of love and enthusiasm.

You would do well governing a large corporation with many employees to oversee. Being a minister, leader of awareness groups, a lecturer or an actor would put your dramatics to good use.

This is an intense vibration to handle, but with your leadership abilities there should be no problem. This range of feeling should give you a wide choice in the selection of a mate or lover. You can be the soft, attentive lover or the firm, passionate and exciting lover—depending on our mood.

33 is a combination of the idealistic **11** and the practical **22**. This means that your concepts would be hard to challenge because you have worked your ideas out in a very practical way to appeal to most people.

NEGATIVE: The most serious negative vibration would be to try to control others through your negative emotions. On another tack you could become cold and uncaring about others. Important decisions need a clear and logical approach; we cannot shirk our duty, becoming uncaring and erratic.

Number 33

Color: Deep sky-blue—for intensity.
Element: Water—for emotional mastery, flowing with or controlling the stream.
Musical Note: High G—for emotional healing. Help people to heal their negative emotions.

DESTINY NUMBER 44

This is the number of the universal builder, Leo, power in high government circles, instituting world-wide reforms for the good of mankind.

Your mental prowess is highest in this number. In our mental processes we use logic to weigh one idea against another. There is the two-valued logic (right or wrong); the three-valued logic (right, wrong or maybe); and then there is simply your side, my side and the correct side. If we take a quantum jump we get to infinite-value logic, "righter" at one time than another or "wronger" at one time than another—infinite distance on either side.

You have the ability to use one of these processes, Leo, or to change in the middle to use another process as you judge your opponent. Your quick mind and confidence can rule over the slower thinkers and deciders.

Your mate or lover would need to be someone who can at least be only one step behind you in intelligence. The challenge would be someone who is one step ahead of you! Anyone for a good fight?

44 is a combination of the idealistic **11** and the **33** which is emotional mastery. This means that the creative, idealistic ideas you have are put forth with emotion (which you control) and feeling to accomplish your goals (**44**).

44 is also the combination of two **22**s, the physical mastery over self. **44** can stand alone as the powerful manifesting number of material goods. Medicine, law, social service or some healing science would put your energies to good use, Leo.

NEGATIVE: If things do not go your way, you can roar like a lion, scaring everyone. You fix on one idea and want to carry it through to its completion, which is positive unless your idea was incorrect—a viewpoint that you find hard to accept.

Number **44**

Color: Blue-green—for tranquility, the magic of speech as well as soft music.
Element: Earth—for mental mastery.
Musical Note: High *A*—for mental healing.

DESTINY NUMBER 55

The divine fire, the eternal flame that is Leo creates the vortex of energy from which life flows. Leo's fire does not stop burning, but the fuel he/she uses determines the quality of the fire. The unevolved Leo feeds on his/her own ego. This "ego" fuel could create a very conceited person. If Leo's fire is fed from vibrations of divine inspiration then he or she becomes a flame with spiritual zeal.

At this level you can become a channel, bringing light and knowledge from higher dimensions into the consciousness of those ready to receive this inspiration.

Think of **55** as being a combination of **22**, the physical and practical master, and **33** the master of emotions. **55** brings these together with the life essence which means that you can learn to understand how to control emotions in a practical way; looking at just where you are and where other people are when they react with exposed emotions to events that transpire on this level of existence—the third dimension. This life energy can elevate the consciousness of all those you contact, Leo, since this fire of leadership is inherent in your sign.

Or you can think of **55** as being the combination of **11**, the idealist, and **44**, the mental master. The idealist provides the creative inspiration that the mental master sets into viable form, then the **55**, Leo, gives life to the project. So you can be creative and practical as you put your project into action (life force).

NEGATIVE: This is the victim, working to decrease knowledge, burning books, repressing the ideas of others, refusing promotions to deserving employees, suppressing action toward expansion, invalidating others as well as self.

Number **55**

Color: Red-violet—the abundant life energy.
Element: Air—for spirituality. Discover the way of the masters. Meditate on your color.
Musical Note: Chord of G—for spiritual healing.

DESTINY NUMBER 66

Use the Research and Discovery method, page 11, to see if this powerful Master Number is hidden in your birthdate, Leo. **66** is love energy, the full realization that one cannot love others until he loves himself and can outpour this feeling to others.

66 is truly the cosmic mother vibration, the double six leading to the 9: $6 \times 6 = 36$; $3 + 6 = $ **9,** which is brotherly love for all mankind. We are not talking about sex, although that is an important part of living; we are referring to the ecstasy that comes over us sometimes in meditation, giving us the feeling that we are truly connected with the cosmos, the Oneness.

Your eagerness to be up front, leading the battle for the right, is not an ego trip in **66**; it is an awareness of the needs of others. You can lead and others will follow your banner, Leo.

NEGATIVE: A negative **66** would gather many people into his camp by selling them on the idea that "this is the only way to salvation." This **66** would use the energy to enslave others, make them do things "in love" that go against our moral codes. Another negative vibration is repressing love for self and for others, keeping family and friends chained to you with, "You don't love me enough!"

Number **66**

Color: Ultra-rose—the fullest expression of love on this planet. Meditate on this color, it will fully open your heart chakra if all the other laws are followed which have led you to this initiation.

Element: Fire—for burning away the dross, getting rid of the unwanted attitudes, habits that keep us from progressing, indulgences that cloud our aura.

Musical Note: Any chord struck in harmony.

26 PAUL AND VALETA RICE

YOUR PERSONAL CHART

Birthdate _____
Birth Number _____
Birth Sign _____
Birth Element _____

This planetary aspect represents the moral excellence and goodness that the soul has achieved in former lifetimes, virtues which will assist a person in this lifetime.

Birth Musical Note _____

Personal Year for 1983 __6__
Personal Year for 1984 _____
Personal Year for 1985 _____
Personal Year for 1986 _____
Personal Year for 1987 _____
Personal Year for 1988 _____
Personal Year for 1989 _____
Personal Year for 1990 _____

Personal Month Numbers:

January _____   July _____
February _____   August _____
March _____   September _____
April _____   October _____
May _____   November _____
June _____   December _____

Challenges:

Major _____ 3
1st Sub-challenge __14__ 4
2nd Sub-challenge __8__ 1

PERSONAL YEAR

The PERSONAL YEAR NUMBER is the vibration that influences your life in any given year. This is a fine focus of JUPITER, the planet of benevolence and idealism. Jupiter showers you with all the good things of life as long as you recognize what the good things are. If you are operating on the negative side of Jupiter, it could lead you into extravagance and greediness.

To obtain this number you add your BIRTH *MONTH* and your BIRTH *DAY* to the year you are seeking. For example: If your birth *date* is July 24, 1945, and you want to find the PERSONAL YEAR for *1981* you do this:

Add 7 (July) to 24 (the *day*) to 1981 = 1994
1994 = 1 + 9 + 9 + 4 = 23; 2 + 3 = 5, the PERSONAL YEAR for the year 1981 for the person with the birth *date* of July 24, 1945.

Do *not* use your own *birth* year; use the year in which you wish to find your PERSONAL YEAR.

PERSONAL MONTH

Still under the influence of that great planet JUPITER, we also find our own PERSONAL MONTH by adding our PERSONAL YEAR to the current month or the month we are seeking.

Example: July 24, 1945 is the birth *date*. We want to find the PERSONAL MONTH for *December, 1981*. Since we have already established the PERSONAL YEAR for this birth date for 1981 as **5**, we simply add the month of December (3) to this number.

5 the PERSONAL YEAR + **3** (December) = **8**. Therefore, the PERSONAL MONTH for the birth date of July 24, 1945 is **8** for December 1981.

Compute your PERSONAL MONTHS and find the interpretations on the following pages.

TABLE OF PERSONAL MONTHS

JUPITER: EXPANSION, UNDERSTANDING, FRIENDLINESS, ABUNDANCE, INSPIRATION, INCREASE, SPUR.

The definitive words for Jupiter listed above captured the essence of the positive side of Jupiter's vibrations. Understand these words by using a good dictionary as you discover the true meaning for yourself. Meditating on all the descriptive words given in this booklet will assist you also.

The NEGATIVE side of the JUPITER vibration is:
EXTRAVAGANCE, INDULGENCE, CYNICISM, GREED.

When we talk about the TIMING of your decisions we need to remember that Jupiter has an influence as well as the vibration of the number that you find for your own PERSONAL MONTH. The interpretations for personal months are as follows:

PERSONAL MONTH 1

A new nine-month cycle of endeavor always starts with the number one month. The **9** month is the ending of this cycle. This month you listen to your own counsel, your own desires to succeed. This is the month to start something depending on your Destiny Number. Use the interpretation of your Destiny Number to go along with any and all of the Personal Month interpretations to order to get a better view of where you are and what to do about it, Leo. This month could also bring about a rebirth of ideas you had in the last 9-month cycle that you dropped for one reason or another. It is easy for you to be enthusiatic and optimistic about your goals. Be a little more specific instead of generalizing and you will be able to pinpoint the direction in which you are supposed to run—for run with the ball you will.

NEGATIVE: Indecision could detract from your natural disposition to move ahead. Also, fabricating the truth in order to push your plans forward could get you into trouble this month. The lowest vibration this month is a tyrannical approach to those under your command.

PERSONAL MONTH 2

This is a good month for you to create the climate of calmness for the settlement of disputes. Use your charm and sexual prowess to accomplish your ideals. Sexual does not mean "sex" in the usual connotation—it means the leonine qualities, the way to attract people and what you want this month. Dress well, expect to meet important people who will further your career, don't be caught with your "slip" showing. It would be a good idea to watch all the fine print in every contract, lease, or any money transaction during this time. Do not let this important perusal of detail be left to your employees or friends. See to it yourself that you look over every paper. There is a peaceful aura that reigns over this month which helps make relationships better. A good month for marriage and love and lovers. Curb your tendency to force love from another and use flowers, epicurean meals and loving attention to attain your desires.

NEGATIVE: This **2** month can bring feelings of extreme sensitivity about yourself, Leo. This is a little inner voice that questions your ability if your goals are slow in coming. Next month may bring the fruition of these goals if you have smoothed your way this month.

PERSONAL MONTH 3

Now you can forge ahead in a straight line toward your goals. Last month was sort of withdrawal from the fray, now you see the light at the end of the tunnel. Inspirations come faster and are more easily put into operation with a **3** vibration. Communicate your desires to others. Tell them your goals for the business or for your family. The future is here, looks bright; the past experiences have just fitted you for this month, it's time to move forward!

NEGATIVE: Your inner self, that voice of little courage, may say, "Things do not look good. The media says, etc., etc., etc." This *is* the time to use your kingship and lead people out of the darkness of doubt much as Alfred Hitchcock leads his readers through the intricacies of mystery stories.

PERSONAL MONTH 4

Since you are determined to succeed, this is one of the best months to put your affairs in order. A lot of details may come up during a **4** month which require close attention. Work toward your projected goals so that you will have time to play a little next month. Concentration is needed. Give attention to your co-workers so they do not detract from your persistence toward your constructive goals, Leo. This is also a month which encourages you to manifest what you want to bring into your life, Leo. You can't always order the universe to give you money, power, etc., that you are entitled to, so you ASK. This is not entirely in your nature, for you prefer to go after what you want.

NEGATIVE: You could get very pushy trying to climb that ladder of success and step on others as you reach for the gold ring. There is jealousy and violence in this number on the very lowest vibration, so keep your temper in check, give your co-workers a purr instead of a growl.

PERSONAL MONTH 5

Look at what you are doing and see if this is the time for expansion. Any kind of adventure, travel to strange places, change of scenery or change of lovers can bring you some exciting experiences. If you have been planning to expand your business or your family a **5** month is the proper time to start. It is not a good time for beginning a business, just for enlarging the one you have already started. This is a period of change, seeing how the other half lives. You might even think about moving to another city or state. Indulge yourself as you can do, Leo. Preen a little, dress well and expect stimulating company, lighten up. You can be the star this month.

NEGATIVE: You might find your new friends so interesting you'll shuck off the old ones. Or you might go the other way and resist change because everything is working so well for you. Okay. Just don't become rigid in your habits. Remain flexible.

PERSONAL MONTH 6

With your tawny mane thrown back, your engaging smile and hearty handshake, you can charm the sandals off an Arab. Your warmth and roaring good humor and confidence bring a good feeling to any gathering. You are usually the star, one way or another, but in this number you will be working for the harmony of the group. You'll bring harmony and peace to diplomatic circles or family squabbles if you have to fight to do it. In this number your family comes first. They would be smart to recognize this power in you and humor some of your erratic moods. Since you want to be first in all things you feel that you can make your own rules, then you want your family or business associates to live up to the rules. A lot of teachers and politicians are Leos because Leo is good at rationalizing plans, authorities, laws and decisions. Since you are so able, it is hard not to be autocratic. You really take care of others although you sometimes complain about carrying everyone's load—don't kid yourself—you enjoy it!

NEGATIVE: You may be interfering where you are not asked, not letting other people make their own mistakes. You disdain help, why not let others refuse also?

PERSONAL MONTH 7

This is a good month to look back and see where your successes were so you can gain from these experiences. We didn't mention the failures as Leos seldom fail in endeavors. That would be a loss of ego, and how can you lose that when you are the king? You accumulate money, goods and ideas, so you can pass this to others, sharing your largesse freely, for you know (in this perfect occult number) that the more you give the more you receive. Leos are fun people. You can also use this month for healing purposes by the **7** mystical approach.

NEGATIVE: You could become skeptical of others' expertise and use humiliation to cut them down to size.

PERSONAL MONTH 8

This power month is loaded with get-rich ambitions and money-making opportunities. All you need is your energetic outlook and commanding bearing to show others how to invest their time, money and vitality to reach whatever goals they have set for themselves. You are very effective in groups or lecturing as you can put forth the ideas in a clear lucid manner, with a little drama thrown in for color. Power, glory and fame (even money) are the rewards of work well presented and accomplished. This will bring you a surge of psychic energy, a validation of your own worth, which, being a Leo, most people do not think you need. They do not know that underneath you may need all the courage you can muster to get up on the platform and deliver.

NEGATIVE: You could hover over your employees or your family, not giving them the opportunity to work out their own way of getting the job done. Your ego bubble is blown if you do not get compliments or rewards of some kind when your work is successful.

PERSONAL MONTH 9

This is the month to ease restrictions on yourself and others in order to achieve the pinnacle you set eight months ago. Finish your most important projects, and if this is not feasible, at least take a good look at what you are doing that is preventing their completion. This is a time for brotherly love, understanding your employer and employees. Take a little time to investigate their motives. There is compassion for children, romantic episodes for couples and humane pursuits for those who pay attention to this **9** influence.

NEGATIVE: You could become selfish and want to keep all the rewards for yourself, even if you haven't earned them—later your innate honesty would come back to haunt you. Avoid being unkind to persons who do not have your ability to charm. Saving money is fine, just be sure that you do not tighten the reins so much you become stingy.

CHALLENGES OF LIFE

CHALLENGES are obstacles we encounter during this lifetime. We are now concerned with the timing of events that stop you from progressing until you understand just what the obstacle is and means.

In the FIRST HALF of your lifetime, you will encounter a SUB or minor challenge which is represented by a number.

In the SECOND HALF of your lifetime, you will encounter a SUB or minor challenge which is represented by a number.

The MAJOR CHALLENGE, also represented by a number, is with you your entire lifetime until you solve the mystery. We accepted these challenges when we decided to incarnate on this planet so that we can strengthen the weak links in our destiny. Recognizing these weak links by finding the negative influences of these numbers will be helpful.

SATURN is the planet known as the DISCIPLINARIAN, the teacher, the door to the initiation and all these good things we shy away from or fear. See Saturn's other side—if you have no game going, no challenge and life proceeds smoothly straight down the road with the same scenery—where is the spice? Understand the good that Saturn brings us. Saturn is connected to the challenges of life.

FIRST SUB CHALLENGE: Subtract the number of your birth MONTH from the number of your birth DAY or vice versa.

SECOND SUB CHALLENGE: Subtract the number of your birth DAY from your reduced birth YEAR or vice versa.

MAJOR CHALLENGE: Subtract the FIRST SUB CHALLENGE from the SECOND SUB CHALLENGE or vice versa. Place all these numbers in your PERSONAL CHART on page 26.

EXAMPLE: August 13, 1924
8   4   7
    4   3   = **4** is the First Sub-Challenge
       1   **3** is the Second Sub-Challenge
                1 is the Major Challenge

TABLE OF CHALLENGES

1—Many people will try to dominate and control your life. The remedy is choosing your own way without being belligerent about it. Know when you are right and please yourself after considering all the facts. Strengthen your self-determinism and be the daring, creative person you really are. Dependence on others can limit your talents.

2—Your feelings are uppermost and you are apt to turn others' opinions into personal affronts. This sensitivity can be very useful if you "tune" into people and see where they are. Cultivate a broader outlook on life and learn to be cooperative without being indecisive. Be thoughtful and consider the welfare of others as well as your own.

3—Social interaction frightens you and your reaction is to withdraw or become the loud overreactor. Each violent swing of the pendulum suggests that you are living in a personal construct without reality. Develop your sense of humor; try painting, dancing, writing or any artistic sort of self-expression that can bring out the real you.

4—This easy challenge is LAZINESS! However it can lead you into a rut where it is too much trouble to get out of that comfortable chair to answer the phone. Finish your cycles of activity and you will find your energy level rising. The other side of this challenge is rigidity. Learn patience and tolerance without becoming a slave.

5—This "freedom" number allows us to progress BUT it does not mean doing anything and everything we desire without paying attention to our responsibilities. There are laws of society and universe that tell us to use moderation, not overindulgence, in sex, drugs, alcohol or food. Organize your life. Recognize duties to family and friends.

6—This idealistic number may lead you into thinking that you have the best of all possible answers and belief systems. Your opinions can be dogmatic where personal relationships are at the crossroads. Do not impose your "perfection" on others. Give willingly of your time and knowledge without suppressing others' creativity. Turn "smug" into "hug."

7—This research and discovery number challenges you to become scientific and analytical. Heed your inner guidance. Develop a patience with existing conditions and make an effort to improve them. Do not stifle your spiritual nature. Your limitations are self-imposed. Cultivate faith in the justice of the general plan of things then seek to better it.

8—Wastefulness is the keyword for **8**. This can be brought about by carelessness or miserliness. A false sense of values, efficiency and judgements can become fetishes in the material world. Use your energies to cultivate good human relationships and avoid greed. Be guided by reason and not by avarice. Honor, glory, fame and money are okay if acquired in the right way.

9—This challenge is rare since it carries the lack of emotion and human compassion. It also means judging others and refusing to understand them because of an inflated ego. The time has come for this person to learn to love and empathize with others.

10—Here is NO or ALL challenges. Study all the NUMBERS above and see if you react to one. You have reached a point in your spiritual development where you can choose which challenge to release. Smooth the edges, learn and know the vibrations of the independence of **1**; the diplomat of **2**; the emotional thrust of **3**; the diligence of **4**; the expansion of **5**; the adjustment of **6**; the wisdom of **7**; the power of **8**; and the Universal Brotherhood of **9**.

If your CHALLENGES are the same as your DESTINY NUMBER, give it very close scrutiny.

NUMBERS

Every number can be expressed on three levels—POSITIVE—NEGATIVE—REPRESSIVE. This does not mean that a person is expressing on all three levels. You can evaluate yourself by observing:

1. How you react in certain situations.
2. What is your chronic emotional tone? Happy, grumpy, short-tempered, enthusiastic, fearful, bored, etc.?
3. Check how the interpretations listed below represent your over-all response to your daily grind.

POSITIVE	NEGATIVE	REPRESSIVE
Certain	Apathetic	Despotic
Enthusiastic	Unsure	Tyrannical
Definite	Antagonistic	Suppressive
Specific	Vacillating	Hostile
Searching	Non-feeling	Violent
Transforming	Covert	Stop Motions
Activating	Resentful	Hateful

This is the reason that people with the same numbers react differently to certain situations and differ in attitude towards themselves and others. You can choose which level you are now on and change your level if you wish to change yourself. You can also change your name or a few letters of your name to bring in the vibrations of your choice.

See our book on Name Analysis—POTENTIAL! This book gives you an in-depth analysis of your personality. It is soon to be available at book stores or can be ordered direct from the Rices.

Number **1**:
POSITIVE: Creative; optimistic; self-determined; creative mind through feeling; can reach a higher dimension of awareness when preceded by a **10**.
NEGATIVE: Indecisive; arrogant; fabricator.
REPRESSIVE: Tyrannical; hostile; ill-willed.

Number 2:
POSITIVE: Sensitive; rhythmic; patient; a lover; restful; a peacemaker; skilled; responsive to emotional appeal with love; protective.
NEGATIVE: Impatient; cowardly, overly sensitive.
REPRESSIVE: Mischievous; self-deluded; hostile.

Number 3:
POSITIVE: Communicative; entertaining; charming; can acquire knowledge from higher beings; inspirational; an intuitive counselor.
NEGATIVE: Conceited; exaggerating; dabbling but never really learning anything exactly; gossiping.
REPRESSIVE: Hypocritical; intolerant; jealous.

Number 4:
POSITIVE: Organizer; devoted to duty; orderly; loyal; able to heal etheric body by magnetism; works on higher levels; endures.
NEGATIVE: Inflexible; plodder; penurious; stiff; clumsy; rigid; argumentative.
REPRESSIVE: Hateful; suppressive; gets even.

Number 5:
POSITIVE: Adventurous; understanding; clever; knows the essence of life; creative mind on the mental level; traveler; creative healer.
NEGATIVE: Inconsistency; self-indulgence; sloppy; tasteless; inelegant.
REPRESSIVE: Perverted; afraid of change; indulgence in drink, food, dope; no sympathy.

Number 6:
POSITIVE: Harmonious; good judgement; love of home and family; balance; cosmic mother; self-realization; the doorway to higher mind through harmony.
NEGATIVE: Anxious; interfering; careless.
REPRESSIVE: Cynical; nasty; domestic tyranny.

Number 7:
POSITIVE: Analytical; refined; studious; capable of inner wisdom; symbolizes the bridge from the mundane to the esoteric; the mystic; able to heal spiritual gaps.

NEGATIVE: Confused; skeptical; humiliates others; aloof; a contender.
REPRESSIVE: Malicious; a cheat; suppressive to self and others.

Number **8**:
POSITIVE: Powerful; a leader; director; chief; dependable; primal energy; can open third eye; money maker; sees auras.
NEGATIVE: Intolerant; biased; scheming; love of power—fame—glory without humility; impatient.
REPRESSIVE: Bigoted; abusive; oppressive; unjust.

Number **9**:
POSITIVE: Compassionate; charitable; romantic; aware; involved with the brotherhood of man; successful; finisher; merciful; humane.
NEGATIVE: Selfish; unkind; scornful; stingy; unforgiving; indiscreet; inconsiderate.
REPRESSIVE: Bitter; morose; dissipated; immoral.

Number **11**: IDEALIST
POSITIVE: Idealistic; intuitive; cerebral; second sight; clairvoyant; perfection; spiritual; extrasensory perception; excellence; inner wisdom.
NEGATIVE: Fanatic; self-superiority; cynic; aimless; pragmatic; zealot.
REPRESSIVE: Dishonest; miserly; carnal; insolent.

Number **22**: PHYSICAL MASTERY
POSITIVE: Universal power on the physical level; financier; cultured person; international direction in government; physical mastery over self.
NEGATIVE: Inferiority complex; indifference; big talker—not doer; inflated ego.
REPRESSIVE: Evil; viciousness; crime on a large scale; black magic.

Number **33**: EMOTIONAL MASTERY
POSITIVE: The idealist with power to command or serve; leader who has emotions under control; constructive emotionally controlled ideas.
NEGATIVE: Erratic; useless; unemotional; not using his/her gifts of sensitivity to others.

REPRESSIVE: Power to work on other people's emotion to their detriment; riot leaders.

Number **44**:   MENTAL MASTERY
POSITIVE: Universal builder with insight; can institute and assist world-wide reform for the good of mankind; can manifest his postulates.
NEGATIVE: Mental abilities used for confusion of worthwhile ideas; twists meanings of great statesmen and very able people for personal use.
REPRESSIVE: Crime through mental cruelty; uses mask of righteousness to do evil; psychotic.

Number **55**:   LIFE ENERGY
POSITIVE: Abundant life; channels from higher dimensions with ease; brings light into existence; student of action; heals using life force.
NEGATIVE: Karma burdened with inaction on the right path; chooses to look backward and wallow in self-pity.
REPRESSIVE: Victim of life; in darkness; no path visible; withdraws; blames others.

Number **66**:   LOVE ENERGY
POSITIVE: Self-realization through love; this love extends from self to others, knowing that one cannot love others unless one knows and recognizes the perfection of one's own soul.
NEGATIVE: Using love as a tool to enslave another; extreme selfishness and possessiveness; refusing love when time and person is correct.
REPRESSIVE: Seeing only the barriers to love; repressing loving attention to others; repressing the need to outpour cosmic love to others.

BIBLIOGRAPHY

Avery, K., *Numbers of Life*, Freeway Press
Bailey, A., *Esoteric Healing*, Lucis Pub. Co.
_____,*From Intellect to Intuition*, Lucis Pub. Co.
_____,*Initiation: Human and Solar*, Lucis Pub. Co.
_____,*Letters on Occult Meditation*, Lucis Pub. Co.
_____,*Problems of Humanity*, Lucis Pub. Co.
_____,*Telepathy*, Lucis Pub. Co.
Campbell, F., *Your Days are Numbered*, Gateway
Diegel, P., *Reincarnation and You*, Prism Pubs.
Fitzgerald, A., *Numbers for Lovers*, Manor Books
Johnson, V., & Wommack, T., *Secrets of Numbers*, Samuel Weiser, Inc.
Jordan, J., *Romance in Your Life*, DeVorss & Co.
_____,*Your Right Action Number*, DeVorss & Co.
Leek, S., *Magic of Numbers*, Collier-MacMillen, Pubs.
Long, M.F., *Growing into Light*, DeVorss & Co.
_____,*Huna Code in Religions*, DeVorss & Co.
_____,*Secret Science Behind Miracles*, DeVorss & Co.
_____,*Secret Science at Work*, DeVorss & Co.
_____,*Self Suggestion*, DeVorss & Co.
Lopez, V., *Numerology*, New American Library, Inc.
Rice, P. & V., *Potential! Name Analysis*, F.A.C.E.
_____,*Timing*, F.A.C.E.
_____,*Triadic Communication*, F.A.C.E.
_____,*Thru the Numbers*, Samuel Weiser, Inc. (a series for each zodiac sign)
Roquemore, K.K. *It's All in Your Numbers*, Harper & Row
Schure, E., *Pythagoras and the Delphic Mysteries*, Welby, R., & Health Research
Street, H., Taylor, A., *Numerology, its Facts and Secrets*, Wilshire Book Co.
Thommen, G. S., *Is this your Day?*, Crown Publishing Co.